BLUFF YOUR WAY
IN
POETRY

NICK YAPP

D1012761

℞
RAVETTE BOOKS

Published by Ravette Books Limited
Egmont House
8 Clifford Street
London W1X 1RB
(071) 734 0221

First printed 1989
Reprinted 1993

Series Editor – Anne Tauté

Cover design – Jim Wire
Printing & Binding – Cox & Wyman Ltd.
Production – Oval Projects Ltd.

CONTENTS

INTRODUCTION

What is Poetry?

In the days before computer typesetting, it was possible to say that any printed matter without right hand margin alignment was poetry. Advancing technology has put an end to such certainty, and we now need a more complicated definition. It's really a question of discovering what Donne, Anon., e.e.cummings, Ovid, Pam Ayres and Percy Bysshe have in common; or what connects the *Epic of Gilgamesh*, greetings card verses, naughty limericks, *Ode to a Nightingale*, *Sing a Song of Sixpence* and *Paradise Lost*.

To do this, the biggest mistake is to look at the end products themselves. There appear to be no similarities whatsoever between a Shakespearian sonnet and a Matsuyaman haiku, between a Milligan couplet and three or four thousand lines of Alexander Pope, between one of Edward Lear's Nonsense Rhymes and the neo-futuristic monologues of Andrei Voznesensky.

Note: Don't worry if a lot of words like 'neo-futuristic', 'polemical', 'panegyric', 'iconoclastic', etc. don't mean anything to you. Just use them in a slightly haughty manner before anyone else does, and then add "Not a word that one would normally think of applying to his (or her) verse, perhaps . . ."

This book concentrates on English poetry, with a nod towards the US. Even so, somewhere, someday, someone will hurl a name at you that you don't recognise, a balladeer of whom you know nothing. This is when you should smile gently, and use one of the following bluffs:-

a) "Yes, I suppose it's about time I rediscovered him (or her)." This implies that you were aware of this poet ages ago, practically before the ink (or blood) dried on the manuscript.

b)   "Too deceptive for me, I'm afraid." This implies that you have seen through the poet's deception, whereas your companion hasn't.
c)   "I'm afraid that my approach to him (her) can only be described as lacklustre." Although you are ostensibly criticising yourself, the implication is that the poet is hardly worth considering.

You can rediscover anybody – Byron, Ogden Nash, Banjo Patterson, even Gertrude Stein (A rose is a rose is a rose is a rose). Here you are using a Compound Bluff technique, suggesting that not only have you known the poet's work since infancy, but that you are constantly re-evaluating poetry, seeking (and finding) new levels of appreciation, new depths of meaning.

'Depths of meaning' is what poetry is all about. All poetry is deep, profound, heavy, bottomless, suffocating, unfathomable. If you can understand it, it isn't poetry – it's verse. And then your appreciation should draw on the language of the wine expert. Verse is 'crisp and dry' like a White Burgundy, or 'sparkling and clear' like a young Champagne. Verse can be about anything. Poetry concerns itself only with the inexorable course of Love, Rejection and Death, although a great many poets don't bother too much with the first two, but hasten to the last.

Poetry is what happens when sensitive people find themselves overcome and have pen and paper to hand. They may be overcome by all sorts of emotions or feelings; love, joy (rare), despair (everyday), wonderment (often faked), the death wish (enormously common), horror, patriotism (outmoded), faith, lust (but only in a caring sort of way) – the list is endless. The source of the emotion may be almost anything; the Bible, a battle, a daffodil, a woman, a man, a bird, sunsets, the smell of frying onions. The reaction is always the same. Out comes the pen and paper, down goes the poem.

Other types of writer don't say: 'I wrote this novel when

6

I was walking along Hadrian's Wall' or 'One night, when I was swimming the Hellespont, I simply had to write this play'. Poets do. The outcome of their jottings may be very long or very short. The works may or may not rhyme. They may or may not scan. It doesn't matter. Because they are verbal responses to surfeits of emotion, they are poetry.

Poets as Bluffers

Four hundred years ago, **Sir Philip Sidney** (poet, wit, scholar, soldier, courtier and gent.) wrote:

> The poet assertyth not, and therefore lyeth not.

It's an interesting remark for two reasons. Firstly, it shows that even in those days poets were using archaic English – 'thees' and 'thous' and 'listeth' and 'lyeth'. Secondly, brave hero and jolly good chap though he may have been, Sir Philip was also a consummate bluffer. Poets are shocking liars, constantly bending and breaking rules and ignoring Truth for the sake of Art.

Rupert Brooke was one of the worst offenders. Thousands can quote from his poem *To Grantchester*, it's one of the Good Old Good Ones of English Verse:

> Stands the church clock at ten to three?
> And is there honey still for tea?

The church clock did stick in Grantchester in 1911, but at half past three, not ten to three. Why the change? Half past three rhymes, it even scans as well. Either Rupert Brooke couldn't wait for his tea, or he simply wanted to bluff for the sake of bluffing. It's a common practice in verse, and is known as 'poetic licence', granting poets a special station not accorded anyone else. A street trader's licence doesn't legitimise untruths or malpractices on the trader's part. A publican's licence doesn't permit the publican to water his beer (see G.K. Chesterton) or falsify the labels on his bottles. A driving licence is not a passport to deceit. But poetic licence allows any and every poet to indulge in regular bouts of bluffing.

And it doesn't stop at the composition of poetry. As a young poet, **John Clare** used to recite his work to groups at markets and fairs. They laughed at his poems until he 'hit upon a harmless deception by repeating any poems over a book as though I was reading it. This had the desird effect. They often praised then and said if I could write as good, I should do.' This, you should maintain, is why poets, above all others, are prepared to pay to see their work in print.

Other examples of bluffing are scattered throughout this slim volume. For the nonce (see Vocabulary), suffice it to say that Browning hated being in England in April and much preferred Italy; that the whole convention of the pastoral – the independent, cheerful, hardy, virtuous peasant, hugely enjoying a life of poverty-stricken, back-breaking grind in a mixture of appalling weathers – is one enormous poetic bluff, delivered by Burns, Clare, Words-worth and Duck (among others); and that Newbolt, Tennyson, Kipling and the Patriotic Poets of the 19th century were wildly inaccurate in their depictions of historical events.

> Come, Bluffer, where's your wits?
> **Edmund Blunden**, *Pillbox*

POETRY LOVER'S PORTMANTEAU

For some people Poetry is Life. They buy books of poetry; they go to poetry readings and performances; they form poetry clubs and societies; they write the stuff and pay to get it published; they care and worry and fuss about poetry.

These are the Poetry Fanatics and you must beware of them. If you live in certain parts of London, the lusher suburbs of other large cities, or towns with literary connections or festivals (Cheltenham, Dorchester, Dorking, Little Gidding), you may find them hard to avoid. They're in the mould of the Ancient Mariner – mad eyes staring, dribble coming out of the corners of their mouths, seeking some poor wretch to whom they can recite at length. If you can't avoid them, you may consider joining them.

1. How to Dress for Poetry

DON'T:
- wear a velvet smoking jacket or thick cord trousers (people will think you're a psychotherapist)
- grow a beard
- (no great poet of the 20th century has sported a beard)
- slap on a beret (people will think you're from the British Legion)
- wear sandals (people will think you couldn't afford a decent pair of trainers, or that you're a Pole on holiday)
- drip around in a silk dressing gown (people will think you're emulating Ivor Novello or Noel Coward, or worse still, Gilbert and Sullivan's Bunthorne).

DO:
- roll your own cigarettes, as messily as possible
- kit yourself out in a Panama hat, white linen jacket, and two-tone brogues (people won't know which poet you evoke, and that will disturb them).

2. How to Treat Poetry Books
The moment you buy a book of verse, mutilate it:
- break the spine
- fold down the corners as though marking pages
- spill some dark brown (or, better, Burgundian red) liquid on it
- tear out a few pages
- scribble dates and obtuse references in the margins.

Most people who buy poetry books never even open them, let alone read them, so, when you turn up with a volume that looks as though Hull Kingston Rovers have been playing with it, you will be regarded with awe.

3. What to Do When Someone Threatens You With a Poem They've Written
The vital thing is to prevent them reading it to you. If they read it, you have to try to listen and then make a comment. So, when they say: 'May I read you my latest *oeuvre*?', say, firmly: "No. Don't do that. I've just spent three days and nights reading The New Apocalyptics and my mind is completely shattered. Do you know The New Apocalyptics, by any chance . . . ?" They won't.

4. How to Behave at Poetry Readings
Increasingly, poetry has become a performance art. You may turn up, quite innocently, at the Festival Hall or the Barbican or the Free Trade Hall or any large theatre, hoping for some foot-tapping, lightweight free entertainment while you guzzle Sur-Real Ale, and find two men (it's always two men) shouting bits of verse at each other

and making strange and obscene noises into hand-held microphones.

There are two strategies open to you:
1. Run away and drink elsewhere.
2. Wait until they appear to have ground to a halt (it may take a very long time), then trot over to them and say how much you enjoyed it and could they please do something of Eleanor Farjeon's?

5. Poetry Competitions

There are an enormous number of these, organised both nationally and locally. Your library will usually have details, but it's no good entering any of them as every poetry competition has about two million submissions even if the first prize is less than a fiver (it usually is). If you feel you must take part, send in a totally inappropriate poem (obscene or blasphemous if it's your local paper or a woman's magazine: coyly sentimental or nauseatingly anthropomorphic if it's the BBC or the National Poetry Society). That way you can trumpet your lack of success to the poetry community by saying "the Philistines" didn't have the guts to consider your stuff.

6. Anthologies

Never admit to having bought any one of the general anthologies of verse (*The Oxford Book of English Verse*, *The Faber Book of English Verse*, *Palgrave's Golden Treasury*, *The Readers Digest Book of Rhymes*, etc.) Be sneering in your approach to them ("One up from *Poems for Under 9-Year Olds*, perhaps . . .").

There are hundreds of different sorts of anthologies, and the bluffer should go full tilt for the most unlikely (French Cowherd Songs, Burmese Love Poetry, CND Battle Cries, Boardroom Ballads, etc.).

The only other way to use anthologies to your advantage is to make a careful note of the compiler and the date of publication. If you talk of Stallworthy's 1973 *Compilation of Love Poetry*, Hadfield's *Sea Verse for Chameleon*

Books in 1940, Weissbort's *Post War Russian* for Penguin in '74, you will be exhibiting knowledge that no one else possesses, which to many poetry buffs (not bluffs) in the Essence of Life.

It doesn't matter how obscure the anthology is, in fact, the more obscure the better. It may be that the only book of poetry you possess is *The Third Ladybird Book of Favourite Nursery Rhymes*, but if you refer to it as Wills and Hepworth's *Folk Verse Anthology* (". . . '62, wasn't it – or '63? . . ."), people can't help but be impressed.

7. Understanding the Vocabulary
Bluffers should realize that poets not only find spelling difficult, they also use words and phrases that the rest of us don't. Here are a few, with translations:

Fain would I	– I'd like to, but I really don't think I can
Lo!	– I say!
Muse	– Poem
Behold	– Look
Ah!	– Oh!
Sith	– Since
Bootes	– Avails
Avails	– Benefits
Methought	– It occurred to me . . .
Roseate	– Pinkish
Hark!	– Please pay attention
Goodly	– Dull
Plentious	– In stock, available
Such an one	– One of them
Doubt you?	– You sayin' I'm lyin'!
Alas!	– Oh dear
Hoarie	– Freezing
For the nonce	– While I'm waiting . . .
Bosome	– Chest, lap, hill, sea bed, schooldays, Heaven – anything but breast.

The Poetic Vocabulary also includes thee, thou, thereto, thy, doth, ye, commeth, whiles, twixt, makyth, fayrest, unto, eeke, begot, wilt, e'en, ere, and heaps of other words whose meaning is nearly obvious; and certain constructions, such as 'much was I', 'quoth he', 'twas so', 'your trumpets sound'. Most of these constructions stem from an understandable desire on the part of the poet to end the line with an easy rhyme: e.g. it's much easier to find a rhyme for 'so' than 'twas', for 'sound' than 'trumpets'.

The other philological vagary of poets is that they find it impossible to make other than classical allusions to certain objects – the sun is always 'Phoebus'; the nightingale, 'Philomel'; a canine, 'Cerberus'; heaven, 'Elysium'; a wedding, 'Hymen'; a tease, 'Nymphe' or 'Nimph'.

You just have to get used to all this.

TWENTY FAMOUS COUPLETS

Unless you wish to aim very high indeed, the safest
foundation for the bluffer in poetry is to have full
knowledge of what most people can merely recollect
hazily. To this end, commit the following twenty couplets
to memory (you know most of them already), remember
where they came from and who wrote them, and use them
at every opportunity. NB: The secret in most cases is to
know the second line of the poem.

1. Oh England is a pleasant place for them that's rich
      and high,
    But England is a cruel place for such poor folks
      as I . . .
    (**Charles Kingsley** – *The Last Buccaneer*)

2. The boy stood on the burning deck
    Whence all but he had fled
    The flame that lit the battle's wreck
    Shone round him o'er the dead . . .
    (**Felicia Dorothea Hemans** – *Casabianca*)

3. A bunch of the boys were whooping it up in the
      Malamute saloon;
    The kid that handles the music-box was hitting a
      jag-time tune;
    (**Robert Service** – *The Shooting of Dan McGrew*)

4. Oh, East is East and West is West, and never the
      twain shall meet,
    Till Earth and Sky stand presently at God's great
      judgement seat . . .
    (**Rudyard Kipling** – *The Ballad of East and West*)

5. Faire stood the Wind for France
    When we our Sayles aduance . . .
    (**Michael Drayton** – *Agincourt*)

6. Come live with me and be my love,
   And we will all the pleasures prove
   (**Christopher Marlowe** – *The Passionate Shepherd
   to his Love*)

7. Not in vain the distance beckons. Forward, forward
   let us range
   Let the great world spin for ever down the ringing
   grooves of change,
   (**Alfred, Lord Tennyson** – *Locksley Hall*)

8. Golden slumbers kiss your eyes,
   Smiles awake you when you rise . . .
   (**Thomas Dekker** – *Golden Slumbers*)

9. Here a little child I stand,
   Heaving up my either hand . . .
   (**Robert Herrick** – *A Child's Grace*)

10. But soon a wonder came to light, that showed the
    rogues they lied:
    The man recovered of the bite, the dog it was that
    died . . .
    (**Oliver Goldsmith** – *Elegy on the Death of a Mad
    Dog*)

NB: The secret here is to remember the first line.

11. To see the world in a Grain of Sand and a Heaven in
    a Wild Flower,
    Hold Infinity in the palm of your hand and Eternity
    in an hour . . .
    (**William Blake** – *Auguries of Innocence*)

12. Wee, sleekit, cow'rin, tim'rous beastie,
    O what a panic's in thy breastie!
    (**Robert Burns** – *To a Mouse, on turning her up in
    her Nest with the Plough, November 1785*)

NB: The secret here is to try to remember what must be
the longest title of any poem.

13. My heart leaps up when I behold
    A Rainbow in the sky:
    So was it when my life began;
    So is it now I am a man;
    So be it when I shall grow old,
    Or let me die!
    The Child is Father of the Man;
    And I could wish my days to be
    Bound each to each by natural piety.
    (**William Wordsworth** – *The Rainbow*)

14. O, young Lochinvar is come out of the west,
    Through all the wide Border his steed was the best:
    (**Sir Walter Scott** – *Lochinvar*)

15. The Assyrian came down like a wolf on the fold,
    And his cohorts were gleaming in purple and gold.
    (**Lord Byron** – *The Destruction of Sennacherib*)

16. The trumpet of prophecy! O, wind,
    If Winter comes, can Spring be far behind?
    (**Percy Bysshe Shelley** – *Ode to the West Wind*)

17. I mount! I fly!
    O grave! Where is thy victory?
    O death! Where is thy sting?
    (**Alexander Pope** – *The Dying Christian to his Soul*)

18. Against the Brydale day, which was not long:
    Sweet Thames run softly, till I end my song.
    (**Edmund Spenser** – *Prothalamion*)

19. Stands the church clock at ten to three
    And is there honey still for tea?
    (**Rupert Brooke** – *To Grantchester*)

20. Here with a Loaf of Bread beneath the Bough,
    A Flask of Wine, a Book of Verse – and Thou.
    (**Edward Fitzgerald** – *The Rubaiyat of Omar Khayyam of Naishapur*)

POETS AND DEATH

An enormous number of poets died strange, heroic or untimely deaths. It's hard to be rhapsodic about these: bluffers are caring people, who don't go around revelling in the fact that **Marlowe**, **Beaumont**, **Fergusson**, **Chatterton**, **Shelley**, **Keats**, **Emily Brontë**, and many others, all died before they were thirty. Say, rather, what a pity it was that **Tennyson**, **Wordsworth**, **Hardy**, **Belloc**, **de la Mare**, **Masefield** and **Graves** lived so long. "Think what they would have accomplished," you can say, "had their energies been concentrated, as Shelley's was, into two or three decades." People won't understand and assume that you must have a point.

However, for those of a morbid disposition, here is a list of poets for whom Death cameth soon rather than late:

Apollinaire, Guillaume 1880-1918
French Cubist poet. Real name Wilhelm Apollinaris de Kostrowitsky. Began writing poetry while in La Santé prison in Paris, where he'd been sent following the theft of a statuette from the Louvre. Died of wounds received in the War.

Byron, Lord George 1788-1824
The Great Romantic. Died of fever after he'd joined the Greek insurgents fighting for freedom and liberation.

Chatterton, Thomas 1752-1770
The Boy Wonder. A child genius who spent most of his short life forging poems. Reduced to despair by his poverty (there's not much of a market for forged poems), he poisoned himself with arsenic while posing to have his picture painted.

Cornford, John 1915-1936
Christened Rupert John after Rupert Brooke, who had just died and had been a friend of his parents. Academically brilliant and politically perceptive. Went to Spain

and was killed by machine gun fire the day after his twenty first birthday. Read *Full Moon At Tierz*.

Fulke Greville, Lord Brooke 1554-1628
Murdered by his servant, one Heywood, who thought himself omitted from his master's will (this always seems such a silly crime – surely the time to murder someone is when you're included in their will).

Garcia Lorca, Federico 1899-1936
Spanish poet and playwright, murdered by the Fascists early in the Spanish Civil War.

Hyde, Robin 1906-1939
Real name Iris Guiver Wilkinson. New Zealand poet who arrived ill in England after travelling through war-torn China, and soon committed suicide.

Keats, John 1795-1821
Died of consumption in Rome. Epitaph (written by Keats):
   'Here lies one whose name was writ in water'.

Marlowe, Christopher 1564-1593
MI5's most famous poet, killed on active service in a pub in Deptford, ostensibly while arguing about the bill. His death shows:
a) nobody should argue about the bill in Deptford.
b) you shouldn't mix poetry with espionage.

Mew, Charlotte 1869-1928
Following her sister's death, and frightened of loneliness and insanity, committed suicide.

Ralegh, Sir Walter 1552-1618
Unfairly tried on charge of plotting against James I, condemned to death, sent to Tower 1603-1616. Released to undertake an expedition to the Orinoco in search of gold. Failed to find any. Re-arrested on the demand of the Spanish ambassador, sent to Tower, wrote more poems. Beheaded.

Roger Roughton ? -1936
Surrealist poet who killed himself in Dublin, but it may
have been an accident – you can never tell with
Surrealists.

Shelley, Percy Bysshe 1792-1822
Like Keats, made the mistake of moving to Italy, and was
drowned while attempting to sail in Lake Spezia.

Sidney, Sir Philip 1554-1586
Joined in an attack on a Spanish convoy at Zutphen and
received a fatal wound in the thigh.

Southey, Robert 1774-1843
Brilliant intellect and poet who died of softening of the
brain. To guard against this is probably the reason why so
many aspiring poets affect floppy hats, berets, boaters,
etc.

Surrey, Henry Howard, Earl of ?1517-1547
Executed for advising his sister to become Henry VIII's
mistress, an arrangement that clearly didn't suit any of
the three parties involved. Henry himself died eight days
later.

Swinburne, Algernon 1837-1909
Born all but dead, he wasn't expected to live an hour, and
was described by his contemporaries at Eton as a 'queer
little elf' and 'a kind of fairy' – nothing was ever proved.
Peculiarly and congenitally unfitted for dissipation, he
gave it a try. Notorious for his interest in de Sade, his
health prevented him from playing an active part. He died
in Putney of pneumonia when the rest of the household
were down with influenza.

Wilmot, John, Earl of Rochester 1647-1680
Court wit and writer of erotic poems, he 'blazed out his
youth in lavish voluptuousness', and quite simply, died of
an excess.

A PANOPLY OF POETS

Early Origins

Since nobody has the slightest idea where, when or why poetry began (i.e. who was the first to be overcome), this is a most fertile field for the bluffer. In poetry, the mists of obscurity lend a mellow fruitfulness to speculation, pretence, and making a very little knowledge go a very long way.

Of course, it's quite possible that one day, an archaeologist digging away in the Lower Omo Falls, Ethiopia will unearth a thirty thousand year old relic with a limerick carved on it, revealing an ape-like wit:

> If ever they come to detect us,
> They'll look at our skulls, and suspect us
> Of walking around
> With our hands off the ground,
> And label us *Homo Erectus*.

Until then, our jumping off point has to be the ancient city of Uruk in Mesopotamia.

About four thousand years ago a Sumerian poet prepared several hundred clay tablets, and then sat down and, in the wedge-shaped cuneiform writing of the day (which is tremendously easy to rhyme, when you come to look at it), wrote *The Epic of Gilgamesh*. This is a long poem about a king who was two parts god and one part man, who lived to be 126 years old, and whose life was spent in a losing battle with what appears to be congenital pessimism – a very suitable subject for a poem. It's full of 'bitter weeping' and 'evil deeds' and 'was it for this I . . .' - the very stuff of poetry for millennia.

Glorious Greeks

Fifteen hundred years later came the next great poem, **Homer**'s *Iliad*, often described as the Bible of Greece. It isn't necessary to read it, just remember that it's about the life and death of the Trojan prince, Hector, and go into raptures about how wonderful it must have been to hear it chanted by minstrels in the halls of kings – you can adopt this approach to all poetry composed before 1500 A.D. The other thing to remember about the *Iliad*, and its sister poem *The Odyssey*, is that they are the only long narrative poems about deeds of valour that you shouldn't describe as 'Homeric'. If you must read one, try *The Odyssey*; it's four thousand lines shorter.

Every four years, at the Panathenaea in Athens, Homer's epics were performed in front of vast audiences by 'rhapsodes', men who carried long sticks and recited poems for a living. If you really want to impress, you could espouse the cause of *Hesiod*, a lesser known Greek poet, whose most famous piece was *Work and Days*, an eight-hundred-line poem about a grumpy farmer, a bit like 'The Archers' in iambic hexameters.

Roman Roots

The father of Roman poetry was **Ennius** (c239-169 B.C.), who is alleged to have said: 'Unless I have the gout, I never write poetry.' In the end, of course, he died of both. Some consider Latin a terser, more forceful and more precise language than Greek, and say that the Roman poets (**Virgil, Seneca, Plautus, Terence**, et al) displayed a constant moral concern and a more clinical attitude to the emotions. The upshot of all this is that Virgil's *Aeneid* is every bit as long as Homer's *Iliad*, but you may, at least, describe the *Aeneid* as Homeric. Be careful, lots of people have heard of the *Aeneid*: fewer people have heard of Virgil's other great work, the *Georgics* which is about farming and the countryside. Bluffers will claim that the C. Day Lewis' translation is poetry itself.

If you wish to adopt a more saucy approach to poetry, let **Ovid** (43 B.C.-17 A.D.) be your Roman poet. A worldly individual, he wrote a great deal of smutty poetry and was eventually banished to Rumania for filth. His most famous works were the *Amores*, the *Heroides*, the *Ars Amatoria*, and the *Tristia*. To show familiarity with his work, you don't have to read any of it: just smirk and roll your eyes a lot.

The most famous Roman poet of them all is **Thomas Babington Macaulay** (1800-1859 A.D.), who wrote the *Lays of Ancient Rome* (don't get excited – 'lay' doesn't mean what you hope it does. See Glossary). His poetry is wonderfully unfashionable now because it's tremendously easy to learn:

> Then out spake brave Horatius,
> The Captain of the Gate:
> 'To every man upon this earth
> Death cometh soon or late'.   *Horatius*

No poetry that's easy to learn has been fashionable for the last fifty years. Hence, he is ripe for reassessment.

Early English

Always remember that English Poetry (as, indeed, all European poetry) began life as ballads, songs and lays, recited by minstrels, troubadours and jongleurs to audiences of mead-quaffing monarchs and exhausted Irish wolfhounds.

The earliest English poetry that we know of is Northumbrian, but written in the language of Wessex. Poets clearly wished their work to be inaccessible even in those days. Many regard *Beowulf* (written by a Christian scribe in 700 A.D.) as the first English poem, but it was preceded by at least three others: *Widseth*, about Continental courts; *Waldhere*, about French heroism; and *The Fight at Finnesburgh*, which is yet another poem about a battle against fearful odds, the sort that Tennyson would have revelled in, and which is bluff from beginning to end. You can say what you like about these three poems:

nobody's ever heard of them, let alone read them. Commit them to memory (the titles will suffice), then disregard anything that purports to be poetry until:

A Wight y-clept Chauceer

Lots of people have heard of Chaucer because he and Shakespeare have long been the two compulsory English poets, so you have to be very careful here. Only recite a couple of lines when you've practised the pronounciation, (preferably with a slight West Country accent) as follows:

Hwann that Arrpril whith hiss sho-re sawta

the drochte of Maarge hath pair-sed to th' rota . . .

The important thing to remember about Chaucer is that his life remains largely a mystery. This gives great scope for bluffing. It is thought that he was employed in the Secret Service for a year, engaged in y-spionage in Flanders from 1376 to 1377, but there is uncertainty about when he was born, whom he married, and what he did for a living (nobody except Tennyson has ever written poetry for a living).

Since he travelled a great deal, you can speculate wildly about possible meetings he had with Boccaccio and Petrarch (the Italian poets), and talk earnestly (all poetry buffs are earnest) about Italian influences on his work; (". . . octosyllabic went right out of the proverbial window, never to return. Couple of glasses of Orvieto under the cypress with Petrarch and it was heroic stanzas all the way . . . seven lines a stanza . . . like the Seven Hills of Rome, d'you see . . ."). Proceed to describe his later phase (". . . settled down in Aldgate and completely revamped his style . . . heroic couplets from then on . . . crowning achievement . . . try to imagine *The Canterbury Tales* in any other form . . . impossible.").

Don't dwell on *The Canterbury Tales*, it's too well known. Talk instead about *The Boke of the Duchesse* ("interesting but immature"), *The Hous of Fame* ("What a shame he never finished it"), and *The Legende of Good*

23

Women ("Which version of the allegorical prologue do you prefer? Bit derivative, don't you think? Ovid's mark all over it").

If all else fails, mention **Thomas Tyrwhitt** (1730-1786) who established the Chaucer canon. Nobody will know what you mean, but they'll all nod wisely.

It's worth remembering, too, that Chaucer created a number of phrases that have passed into general usage: 'Mordre wil out', 'the smyler with the knyf under the cloke', 'trouthe is the hyeste thing that man may kepe', 'as lene was his hors as is a rake', 'he was a verray parfit gentil knight', 'the lyf so short, the craft so longe to lerne', 'right as an aspen leef she gan to quake', 'entente is al, and nought the lettres' – the trouble is, he couldn't spell.

Edmund Spenser ?1522-1599

Poets were so discouraged by the success of Chaucer that it took two hundred years for the next one to make a name of any sort and even he spent his whole life doing things reluctantly. He reluctantly went to live and work in Ireland, where he wrote much of his best-known poem *The Faerie Queene*. Some hold Spenser as great a poet as Chaucer, and certainly his spelling was a lot better. Unfortunately, several books of *The Faerie Queene* were burnt when Spenser's castle at Kilcolman was set on fire by the locals in 1598. Spenser reluctantly returned to London, where he became reluctantly very poor and very soon died.

Like most 16th century poets, Spenser oozed admiration for Elizabeth I, and *The Faerie Queene* would have been an interminable tribute to her if the good people of Kilcolman hadn't had the sense to burn such a lot of it. It fills six books – Spenser intended eighteen. Like any poem of such length, it is monotonous, though Spenser did invent a new form of stanza, in which a ninth line of twelve syllables is added to eight lines of ten syllables, with a rhyming scheme of abab/bcbc/c.

You may well already know a line of Spenser:

Sweet Thames! run softly till I end my song

which comes from the poem *Prothalamion*. Everyone else will think it is some kind of drug, so you can chatter at length about its being written (reluctantly) in 1596 to celebrate the double marriage of Lady Elizabeth and Lady Katherine Somerset (not to each other, you understand).

Numerous Knights

The 16th century also saw a vast number of knights and nobles writing verse in between voyaging round the world, dying heroically in foreign fields and having their heads cut off, though their poetry was seldom that bad. The best known are **Sir Thomas Wyatt**, **Sir Walter Raleigh**, **Sir Philip Sidney**, **Henry Howard Earl of Surrey**, and **Fulke Greville (Lord Brooke)**.

Wyatt was one of Anne Boleyn's lovers, but timed his affair wisely, e.g. before her marriage to Henry VIII. The only memorable line of poetry he wrote was

And wilt thou leave me thus?

which he reckoned was so good that he used it several times.

Few know that **Sir Walter** really spelt his name **Ralegh**. It's advisable to abide by this, as by his time even poets' spelling had improved beyond all recognition, though they still had trouble with 'desyre', 'promysse', 'despayre', and went completely to pieces with 'ioye' (=eye). The night before he died, Ralegh wrote a clever and moving poem, referring to his execution with a wit and frankness that can't have been easy. It's worth reading.

Sir Philip Sidney was one of a group who formed the Areopagus Club for the purpose of naturalising the classic metres in English verse. He is remembered for two things – passing up a drink as he was dying on the battlefield of Zutphen ('Thy necessity is yet greater than mine') and writing several famous poems, most of which begin with the letter A (*Arcadia, Apologie for Poetrie, Astrophel*, atcetera.

He also wrote a prose work about poetry – *The Defence of Poesy* – in which he attacked some of the lesser bards of his time:

'There have been many most excellent poets that have never versified, and now swarm many versifiers that need never answer to the name of poets.'

Sublime Shakespeare

There are two vital pieces of information about Shakespeare. First, that he wanted to be remembered as a poet only. Second, that he didn't write a great deal of poetry: *The Rape of Lucrece, Venus and Adonis, The Phoenix and the Turtle* and over one hundred and fifty (CL) *Sonnets*.

The Rape of Lucrece is a poem of seven lined stanzas on the subject of Lucretia, whose beauty inflames Sextus, son of the King of Rome, to such an extent (so he says) that he can't control himself. Lucretia commits suicide, and the entire Tarquin family is booted out of Rome and replaced by a republican government. *Venus and Adonis* is a poem of six-lined stanzas, probably Shakespeare's first published work, about the inability of Venus to dissuade the youthful Adonis from going hunting and getting himself killed by a wild boar – serves him right. *The Phoenix and the Turtle* is a mocking, tragic poem – possibly about a mock turtle and a mock phoenix – both of whom perish in their love. Be warned: very few of Shakespeare's poems, or anybody else's for that matter, have happy endings.

But it is *The Sonnets* that are his finest verse works. Published in 1609, and probably written between 1593-96, they fall into several groups. Nobody is quite sure whether they are dedicated to the Earl of Pembroke or the Earl of Southampton – but it would seem that Nos. XL to XLII refer to a 'stolen mistress'; Nos. LXXXIII to LXXXVI to a 'rival poet'; and No. CXXVII onwards to a 'dark beauty loved by the author'.

Whereas his plays are seemingly famous quotations held together by bits of plot, there are few well known quotations from *The Sonnets*, apart from No. XVIII:

Shall I compare thee to a summer's day?

Pick a number, any number, learn a few lines other than the first, and look knowledgeable.

Donne and Milton

John Donne, ex-Roman Catholic, secret marrier, part-time soldier, Anglican cleric and great preacher, was the greatest of the 'metaphysical poets', writing verse in which passion and reason are disappointingly inter-woven. This is exemplified in one line from his poem *The Cannonization*:

For God's sake hold your tongue, and let me love.

But, of course, Donne couldn't hold his tongue. No poet has ever been able to do this. So reason keeps interfering in what could otherwise be quite exciting stuff.

Milton's poetry is excellent if you don't try to read more than twelve lines without a break of at least three weeks.

Having been secretary to Cromwell, Milton was arrested at the Restoration and heavily fined. Shortly afterwards, understandably, he wrote *Paradise Lost*. Things picked up financially and he wrote *Paradise Regained*. Nobody knows why he wrote *Samson Agonistes*, so you can have a field day here. In the end he did better than most poets since the Roman Ennius, and managed to die of gout.

Restoration Poets

The names to look out for are **Herrick**, **Waller** (Edmund, not Fats), **Butler**, **Marvell**, **Dryden** and **Anon**.

Herrick's poetry appears highly horticultural:

Fair daffodils we weep to see . . .

I sing of brooks, of blossoms, birds and bowers . . .

Cherry ripe, ripe, ripe, I cry . . .

but is really extremely sensuous. Even one of his most famous 'flowery' lines:

Gather ye rosebuds while ye may . . .

is the opening of a poem entitled *To the Virgins, to make much of Time* and his other titles include: *On Julia's Legs* (Fain would I kiss my Julia's dainty leg . . .), *No Difference i' th' Dark* and *Delight in Disorder* (A sweet disorder in the dress, kindles in clothes a wantonness).

Waller managed to avoid being executed by the Round-heads by betraying all his Royalist associates (probably in heroic couplets) and spent the rest of his life writing poems of polished simplicity and fawning gratitude to whomever was in power: *Panegyric to My Lord Protector, His Majesty's Escape At St. Andere*. On the side, he wrote several poems in praise of various women.

Butler has the distinction of being the first poet to make a reference to 'punk':

And made them fight, like mad or drunk

For Dame Religion as for punk . . .

This comes from his best known poem, *Hudibras*, for which he was given a lump sum of £300 and a pension of £100 a year by Charles II, making it jolly hard for Butler to die in penury, but, like most poets, he managed to do so.

Marvell was first a poet and later an MP – most people try this progression the other way round. In the former capacity he wrote many poems in praise of gardens and country life, thus beginning a trend which has unhappily flourished among versifiers ever since. His best known work may be his *Horatian Ode upon Cromwell's Return from Ireland*, which goes so far in eulogising the warty General that it's hard to believe it isn't sarcastic:

(The Irish) can affirm his praises best,

And have, though overcome, confest

How good he is, how just,

And fit for highest trust.

Such sycophancy could only lead to a career in politics. Marvell became MP for Hull.

John Dryden was the first official Poet Laureate, though not all his poetry is bad. He wrote an enormous number of poems, many of them unreadably long, but you could try dipping into *Absalom and Achitophel* (only a few thousand lines long) or *Alexander's Feast* (sometimes known as the *Second Song for St Cecilia's Day*), which contains perhaps his best known line:

> None but the brave deserves the fair

or *MacFlecknoe*, a satirical work that attacks one of Dryden's contemporaries, a poet with the less than lyrical name *Shadwell*. In Dryden's poem, Shadwell's pre-eminence in the realm of dullness leads him to being crowned at the Barbican, which shows remarkable foresight on the part of Dryden. He was clearly a man not without wit, but translating the entire works of Virgil must do something to you.

The best poems of the early period, however, were written by the famous **Anon**, and include *Sir Patrick Spens* (which reads like a Will Fyfe monologue), *Greensleeves* (one of Henry VIII's favourite poems), and ballads such as *Robin Hood and Allan a Dale*. A ballad is a simple poem, usually spirited, invariably understandable, written in short stanzas and narrating a popular story. Bluffers should point out the shame that we seldom know who wrote poems that are understandable, but always know who wrote the incomprehensible, and suggest that it probably has something to do with the Meaning of Life.

Gothic Revival

This term refers to a part of the 18th century when many writers became obsessed by the frightening and supernatural. It's an exciting phrase, perhaps a desperate attempt to make 18th century poetry sound interesting. It isn't.

All the poets of the 18th century are incredibly dull: **Pope, Thomson, Johnson, Gray, Goldsmith, Cowper** and a host of others. Don't bother with any of them. They spent half their time writing dull verse, and the other half criticising the dullness of others. Thomson moves a little away from the artificiality of most of them, but is to be forever condemned for writing *Rule Britannia*. Johnson's poems are as leadenly witty as was his conversation. Gray wrote two poems that get into every anthology and from which everyone can quote. Goldsmith wrote one poem (*The Deserted Village*) from which most are familiar with:
And fools, who came to scoff, remained to pray.

Cowper was bullied at school, tried to commit suicide, and wrote *John Gilpin* to divert himself from melancholia. He didn't succeed. With the exception of **Chatterton** (see Poets and Death) none of the 18th century poets managed to die in an interesting way. Despite this, you could commend five poems from this period:

1. *Tom Bowling* by **Charles Dibdin**. Not only a rattling good poem, but a most moving song. George II was so moved that he granted Dibdin a lump sum of £1000 and a pension of several hundred pounds a year, simply for writing this one work.
2. *The Tyger* by **William Blake**. Dreadfully spelt, but wonderfully written.
3. *Jerusalem*, also by **Blake**. Moves even atheists.
4. *Tam o'Shanter* by **Robert Burns**. Impossible to understand unless you speak old Scots, but none the less enjoyable for a' that.
5. *A Red, Red Rose*, also by **Burns**.

With the possible exception of **Dibdin** these poets are well known and many will write off their work as mere songs or popularist, lightweight stuff. What the bluffer needs do, therefore, is approach the poems in a solemn and heavyweight fashion. Point out, for example, that in *Jerusalem*, we have a clear exposition of **Blake**'s Theory of Imagination, "the real and eternal world of which the Vegetable Universe is but a faint shadow". People will start thinking of parsnips and won't understand, which is the secret of talking about poetry.

In the case of **Burns** make much of the conflict within him: sympathy with the ardour of the French revolutionaries on the one hand, but a propensity to convivial living on the other. Suggest how different things would have been had he taken passage to Jamaica as he planned at the age of 27. He could have been the first Scottish reggae poet and rapper. If all else fails, just recite the odd line of Burns – you'll be amazed:

a) how much of it you know already
b) how quickly the room is cleared.

As your trump card, have ready the information that neither Blake nor Burns ever went to school.

The Romantics

Whereas everyone remembers the names of the 18th century poets but can't remember their poems, nobody remembers the names of the Romantic Poets but everyone remembers their poetry:

The Lay of the Last Minstrel
The Bishop Hatto and the Rats
The Minstrel Boy
Abu Ben Adhem
The Burial of Sir John Moore at Corunna.

The Romantics managed to lead appropriately romantic lives. **Leigh Hunt** was imprisoned for writing a critical article on the Prince Regent in 1813, and also brought about the meeting of **Keats** and **Shelley**. **Moore** accumulated debts of £6000 in Bermuda and managed to pay them off. **Scott** ran up debts of £114,000 and worked himself to death in an attempt to pay his creditors. **Southey** was expelled from Westminster School for a precocious essay against flogging, spent a life stuffed with domestic misfortunes and died of softening of the brain. **Wolfe** died romantically young, at the age of 32, and some have unkindly called his most famous poem (*The Burial of Sir John Moore*) a 'mere freak of intellect'. **Byron** liked the poem but reckoned that someone else, probably Campbell, wrote it, and there has been dispute over the authorship ever since.

The Giants of Poetry (or The School of Ill Health)

Apart from the Lake Poets, the Giants of English Poetry are **Byron**, **Shelley** and **Keats**, who between them managed only 92 years of life. When you consider that **Tennyson** lived to be 83 all on his own, you can appreciate the full truth of Defoe's couplet:

The best of men cannot suspend their fate
The good die early, and the bad die late
(Character of the late Dr S. Annesley)

George Gordon Byron 1788-1824

Most of Byron's poetry is described by experts as Byronic, which shows how easy it is to be an expert on poetry. 'Byronic' means rebelling against the conventional morality, defying fate, being contemptuous of the Society that Byron scorned and left. But Byron's poetry was also proud, moody, cynical, defiant, full of revenge, often deeply moving and beautiful. Byron's great gift was to write immensely long poems which are also totally readable, but you could go for something short like *She walks in Beauty*, only eighteen lines and every one a winner.

Percy Bysshe Shelley 1792-1822

Shelley, too, led a romantic life. He was sent down from Oxford in 1811 for writing a pamphlet entitled *The Necessity of Atheism*. He married at the age of 18 and again at 24, after his first wife drowned herself in the

Serpentine. His poetry is ferocious and beautiful, and he used it to great effect in his attacks on Castlereagh's Tory administration (*The Mask of Anarchy*) and George IV's matrimonial affairs (*Oedipus Tyrannus*, or *Swellfoot the Tyrant*). It seems a shame that he's remembered, via English Literature syllabi, chiefly for his softer, admittedly graceful poetry, such as *Ode to the West Wind*, *Ozymandias* and *To a Skylark*.

John Keats 1795-1821

The wonder is that Keats wrote any poetry at all in his short life, ravaged by consumption and nursing his brother, Tom, whom he loved and who predeceased him by three years. But Keats wrote several long poems (*Endymion*, *Hyperion*, and *Lamia* – all of them subsequently made into famous racehorses), some of the finest odes in the English language (*To a Nightingale*, *To Autumn*, *To a Grecian Urn*), and some forty sonnets (*To XXXXX*, *On First Looking into Chapman's Homer*, *On the Grasshopper and Cricket*, *To J.R.* – no, a different J.R. and *To Sleep*).

Be unstinting in your praise of Keats, who received only bad reviews in his short lifetime (at the hands of the Tory press because he was a friend of **Leigh Hunt**), and who has received only glowing tributes since his death.

The Lake Poets

Strictly speaking, **Robert Southey** is regarded as a Lake Poet, but the most famous are **William Wordsworth** and **Samuel Taylor Coleridge**, who met in their early twenties and formed a long-lasting friendship. Wordsworth was an early supporter of the French Revolution, wrote some wonderful poems (*Lines Composed Above Tintern Abbey*, *Sonnet on Westminster Bridge*, *The Solitary Reaper*, and *The Lyrical Ballads*) and then went all to pieces and ended up as Poet Laureate.

Coleridge led a more interesting life, with the help of opium, but wrote less revered poetry than Wordsworth.

Nowadays, people remember only *The Rime of the Ancient Mariner* and *Kubla Khan*. As young men Coleridge and Southey devoted themselves to Pantisocracy, which sounds dirty but was in fact a form of Communism which they intended to practise on the banks of the Susquehanna River in Pennsylvania, where, presumably, no one would see them. The project never got off the ground.

Wordsworth spent the years 1804 to 1806 in the Lake District writing *The Prelude*, an enormously long autobiographical poem. Coleridge spent the years 1804 to 1806 in Malta and Italy, becoming an opium addict. You have to decide which had the better time.

Jingo Lingo

The 19th century is crammed with poets fighting to declaim their patriotic fervour: **Macaulay**, **Tennyson**, **Newbolt**, **Austin**, **Kipling** and scores of other lesser known and even worse poets.

Thomas Babington Macaulay 1800-1859

Another MP and poet, Macaulay's poems are all about heroes and heroines, and battles, some of them amazingly awful:

They are here:- they rush on,- we are broken:- we are
   gone:-
Our left is borne before them like stubble on the blast,
O Lord, put forth thy might! O Lord, defend the right!
Stand back to back in God's name, and fight it to the last.

Maybe he was a good MP.

Alfred, Lord Tennyson 1809-1892

Not all Tennyson's poetry is awful, which is surprising when you realize that:
a)   he became Poet Laureate,
b)   he was given a pension of £200 by Sir Robert Peel
c)   Queen Victoria thought he was wonderful.

Try to forget *The Revenge*, *The May Queen* and *The Defence of Lucknow*, and concentrate on *Crossing the Bar*, *Locksley Hall* (In the spring a young man's fancy lightly turns to thoughts of love), and *Morte d'Arthur*.

Sir Henry Newbolt 1862-1938

So bad, he's essential. Newbolt should have been Poet Laureate, and may well have spent his entire adult life believing that he was. Read all his poems, learn them by heart, they will take away the very breath of any expert or critic – viz: *Clifton Chapel*:

> To set the cause above renown,
> To love the game beyond the prize,
> To honour while you strike him down,
> The foe that comes with fearless eyes.

Many of Newbolt's poems have been set to music (*Drake's Drum*, *The Old Superb*) which makes them even better. You can sing them at the critics and intellectuals.

Robert Bridges thought *Drake's Drum* wonderful – 'I wish I had ever written anything half as good' – which tells you all you need to know about Robert Bridges. Newbolt's poetry was amazingly popular. *Admirals All* ran to four editions in a fortnight in 1897.

Alfred Austin 1835-1913

Austin was by and large an unsuccessful poet with an understandably wavering faith in his poetic genius. He was a man of forthright political views – he rejoiced in Prussia's success in 1870, thought Garibaldi 'an unmitigated nuisance', and wrote a most unfortunate ode celebrating the Jameson Raid. Austin worked on the principle that no poem could be great unless it was an epic on a theme combining love, patriotism and religion (you'd be amazed how many poems do).

Rudyard Kipling 1865-1926

Many people are astonished to learn that Kipling won the Nobel Prize for Literature in 1907, but then they probably haven't read the Polish novels of H. Sienkiewicz, who won the prize in 1905, or the Italian poems of Giosue Carducci, who won the prize in 1906. The point is, it's not essential to write off Kipling's poetry simply because it scans and rhymes. Point out that his work is all quotations:

> For the female of the species is more deadly
>   than the|male . . .
> What stands if Freedom fall? . . .
> Who die if England live? . . .
> 'It's clever, but is it Art?' . . .
> To the legion of the lost ones,
> To the cohort of the damned . . .
> You're a better man than I am, Gunga Din . . .
> . . . the flannelled fools at the wicket or the
>   muddied oafs at the goals . . .
> On the road to Mandalay . . .
> The Captains and the Kings depart . . .
> Brandy for the parson . . .
> Sussex by the Sea . . .
> Take up the White man's burden . . .

> The whole of the poem *If*.

The trouble with Kipling was that he lived a reasonably long time and died from natural causes, which precludes him from being a great poet.

Other 19th Century Genii

Apart from the **Brownings** and the **Rossettis**, who came in couplets, most other 19th century poets were part-timers. Novelist poets included **Thackeray**, **Emily Brontë**, **Kingsley**, **Matthew Arnold**, **Meredith**, **Hardy** and **R.L. Stevenson**. **William Morris** wrote poetry when he wasn't wallpapering; **Lewis Carroll** wrote poetry when he wasn't doing sums; **Edward Lear** invented the limerick; **Oscar Wilde** wrote poetry when he wasn't being delightfully outrageous with a hock and seltzer.

Probably the most famous thing the Brownings did was to elope, but **Robert Browning** also wrote *The Pied Piper of Hamelin*. Most people know the story of the first two-thirds of the poem but forget that, at the end, the children emerge into Transylvania. There is a great deal of wit in the poems of Robert Browning, and a great deal of beauty in the poems of **Elizabeth Barrett Browning**, especially in her *Sonnets from the Portuguese*. Unlike most poets, the Brownings lived more excitingly than they died.

You could suggest that the most interesting poet of his time was **Gerard Manley Hopkins** (1844-1889) who wrote such naughty poetry that none of it was published until thirty years after his death, which is a sure-fire but rather disappointing way of becoming a cult figure. He was first moved to writing poetry at the age of 31 by reading of the death of five nuns in a shipwreck, which is scarcely surprising since he was a priest. Hopkins is best known for his technique ('sprung rhythm') which relates to his sensual poems, not to his sensual life. Refer to 'inscape' (the essence of an object) and 'instress' (what happens when inscape is understood by the reader).

War Poets

Brooke, Thomas, Rosenburg, Charles Sorley, Owen, T.E. Hulme, Leslie Coulson, Jeffery Day, Julian Grenfell, W.N. Hodgson, T.M. Kettle, Francis Lethwidge, John MacCrae, E.A. Mackintosh, R.B. Marriott-Watson, Nowell Oxland, Robert Palmer, Alan Seeger, Patrick Shaw-Stewart, E.W. Tennant, R. Everriede, T.P. Cameron Wilson are just some of the poets that fought and died in the First World War. They were all young, egocentric, talented and almost forced into verse by the horror of their experiences. Some critics have suggested that it was the static nature of their nightmare existence, creating a fruitful routine, that accounts for the excellence of the poetry of this time –

fewer poems written in the Second World War are reckoned in the same class.

Edmund Blunden, himself a soldier in the War, reckoned that the term 'War Poet' was inaccurately applied to many of his contemporaries. Some (**Brooke**, **Sassoon**, **Thomas**, **Graves**, **David Jones**) were poets who happened to be caught in Armageddon, but whose work encompasses many other themes. Others, like **Owen**, had time to write only of war.

Because of the success and fame of the War Poets of 1914-1918, a cry went up at the beginning of the 1939-1945 War: 'Where are the War Poets?' Cyril Connolly's sharp retort was 'Under Your Nose', and the dreadful days of death once again produced some of the best poetry of the century. They also brought about the death of scores more poets: **Drummond Allison**, **Brian Allwood**, **David Bourne**, **Clive Branson**, **Timothy Corsellis**, **Keith Douglas**, **James Farrar**, **Keith Foottit**, **Stephen Haggard**, **T.R. Hodgson**, **John Jarmain**, **David Geraint Jones**, **Sidney Keyes**, **Alun Lewis**, **David Raikes**, **Richard Spender**, **Gervase Stewart**, **Frank Thompson** (publicly executed at the age of 23 in South Serbia, after fighting with the Bulgarian partisans) and **Nigel Weir**. Many of them were young pilots in the RAF, and there is an amazingly calm premonition of death in their work. It should also be remembered that a great many other (sometimes better known) poets were writing during and after the Second World War – **John Arlott**, **Charles Causley**, **Paul Dehn**, **Gavin Ewart**, **Laurie Lee**, **John Lehmann**, **Louis MacNeice**, **Henry Reed**, **Stephen Spender**, **Dylan Thomas** and **Henry Treece** (one of The New Apocalyptics) among them.

Modernism

Modern poets are those who have decided that the secret of writing verse is not to write verse, but to chop up prose and distribute the pieces unfairly

> So that
> One line may contain a great many syllables,
> And another,
> One.

The impact of Modernism is such that the only poetry written in the last fifty or sixty years that both scans and rhymes is either meant to be funny or commercial.

In order to stop modern poets sneering at you as they roll their cigarettes or fiddle with their earrings, you should be able to speak earnestly about the various types of modern poetry. It isn't difficult: think of almost any word that ends in -*ism* (except 'rheumatism' or 'criticism') and throw it into the conversation as you would bean-sprouts into a wok – **Imagism, Dadaism, Existentialism, Surrealism, Symbolism, Movementism, Vorticism**. It helps, of course, if you have some vague idea as to what these terms mean, and many of them, though not all, do have a meaning.

Imagism
Founder: **Ezra Pound**.
Proponents: **Richard Aldington**, **'H.D.'** (Hilda Doolittle – nothing to do with the Doctor), **F.S. Flint** (nothing to do with the Captain), **Skipton Cannell**, **Amy Lowell**, **William Carlos Williams**, **Ford Madox Ford** (extra points if you refer to him as Ford Madox Hueffer), **Allen Upward**, and **John Cournos**.
Floreat: 1910 to 1918 (renewed briefly in the late 1920s).
Characteristics: Anglo-American. Influenced by Chinese, Japanese and early Greeks. Purity of diction. Mercifully small poems. Precision of imagery (hence Imagism).

Technique: 'Direct treatment of "the thing", whether subjective or objective; to use absolutely no word that did not contribute to the presentation; as regarding rhythm – to compose in sequence of the musical phrase, not in sequence of a metronome.' (*Poetry* (American magazine) March 1913).

It doesn't matter if you don't understand what this means: no one would dare ask you to explain.

Dadaism
Founder: **Tristan Tzara**.
Proponents: Few, though the **Sitwells** show a little lighthearted influence.
Floreat: 1917 to 1922.
Characteristics: The aim of Dada was to be destructive and to deny sense and order, to suppress all logical relationship between ideas by violence and/or a savage, comic irony.
Technique: Sit down, write anything you like and eventually an idea or theme will emerge. A godsend, therefore, to all of us without talent. It's a wonder the movement lasted only five years.

Existentialism
Founder: **Kierkegaard**, though there have been existential punch-ups between supporters of rival candidates, and those who assert that Existentialism can't have a founder.
Proponents: **Sartre, Heidegger, Marcel, Camus** and **Jaspers**.
Floreat: 1920s to the present.
Characteristics: Emphasis on uniqueness of human experience and essential individuality of life. French flavour, eclectic, full of disgust for the world. Concerned with feelings, most of them unpleasant.
Technique: Most existential writing has to include:

a) someone dying, preferably of suppurating boils,
b) someone being sick,
c) someone being bored out of his or her mind,
d) someone being hideously poor,
e) everyone contemplating suicide.

Surrealism
Founder: (Off shoot of the Dadaists).
Proponents: (In England) **David Gascoyne**, **Francis Scarfe**, **Roger Roughton**, **Philip O'Connor**. (In France) **André Breton**, **Paul Eluard**, **Louis Aragon**.
Floreat: Mid 1920s to mid 1930s.
Characteristics: Hatred of the prevailing system, exploration of the unconscious mind, rational principles.
Technique: Automatic writing (as in Dadaism). It's hardly surprising that Surrealism is now discredited by all except producers of Arts programmes for the BBC.

Symbolism
Founder: **Baudelaire**.
Proponents: **Mallarmé** and **Verlaine** – not a French department store, but two poets – and an enormous number of Russian poets, all of whose first names are Vladimir – **Solovyov**, **Bryusov**, **Ivanov**, **Etceterov**.
Floreat: 1880 to 1890+
Characteristics: 'A symbol of the verbal parallel to a pattern of experience' (Kenneth Burke, American critic). The aim of Symbolism is to evoke, rather than describe.
Technique: Impressions, intuitions, sensations. All the symbolists did was to liken life to objects – Life is a clockwork toy, a raspberry jelly, a chicken nugget . . .

Movementism
Not strictly a term at all, most people refer to it as The Movement.
Founder: There isn't a founder, since The Movement is discerned rather than established.

Proponents: **Philip Larkin**, **John Wain**, **Donald Davie**, **Robert Conquest**, **Thom Gunn**, **Kingsley Amis**.
Floreat: 1950s to present.
Characteristics: Tough, ironic, down-to-earth, unsentimental.
Technique: Use of precise language and a rejection of the over-blown, flowery phrases of Romanticism. The Movement seems finally to have broken the Ancient Greek yoke that had previously bruised the shoulders of English poetry from Chaucer to Rupert Brooke.

Vorticism
Founder: **Wyndham Lewis**.
Proponent: **Wyndham Lewis**.
Floreat: 1914 to 1915.
Characteristic: A kind of literary Cubism in which all Art was to be related to the Machine and modern industrialisation.
Technique: Egocentric concern for **Wyndham Lewis**.

Concrete Poetry
Founder: **Apollinaire**.
Proponents: Too many to list – the best known British concrete poet is probably **Ian Hamilton Finlay**.
Floreat: 1900 to present.
Characteristics: Emphasis on the physical existence of the poem – what it's written or printed on, the typography used, any artistic embellishments or decorations. Sometimes accompanied by music – this is invariably the worst type.
Technique: To build rather than to write a poem. Since it may be carved in stone or wood, or have metal words welded together, this is a poem you can actually own, and stick in your garden.

CHOOSE YOUR BLUFF

In addition to a grasp of poetry's origins and development, bluffers should have a nodding acquaintance with one or more of the following groups or schools.

Crossing the Rubicund

The popular image of a poet is of some skeletal, consumptive figure, dying of starvation in a garret, and, when you read most poets' work, it's easy to see why this is such a popular and attractive image. But a select few have combined girth with verthe, and most of them wrote what may be described as accessible poetry. Tennyson was a large man. Masefield worked as a deckhand on the old sailing ships.

At the turn of the century there flourished a beefy bevy of poets – notably **Wilde**, **Chesterton** and **Belloc**. What they lacked in physical dexterity, they made up for in metrical fluency and agility.

Oscar Wilde's most famous poem is *The Ballad of Reading Gaol*. It's still a powerful blast against capital punishment and it still generates hot tears of passion at the thought of Wilde's imprisonment. All of Wilde's poetry is a delight to read – you could almost believe that he wished to communicate with his readers, which, sadly, would preclude him from being a great poet.

Gilbert Keith Chesterton was very large and red, and was ill-inclined to stand for any nonsense. He called a sponde, a sponde. His poetry is shot through with sentiment and religion and a rich thirst. He used his poetry to express his forthright views on almost every subject, and became very popular thereby. It's hugely unfashionable to espouse his poetry today – it would be like whistling a bit of Eric Coates in the queue for a Prom on Boulez Night.

Hilaire Belloc not only wrote poems which are understandable, he even wrote poems which are funny: *The Bad Child's Book of Beasts*, *More Beasts for Worse Children*, *The Modern Traveller*, and, his best known, *Cautionary Tales*, e.g.

> Willie in one of his brand new sashes
> Fell in the fire and was burned to ashes
> And now although the room grows chilly
> We haven't the heart to poke poor Willie.

The Good Old Good Ones

The Rubaiyat is one of those many poems that all have heard of, many have read, few can quote and none can recite. The bluffer can steal a march on others with the verse equivalents of the Golden Oldies by referring to Twenty Famous Couplets, or quoting from this list of the Good Old Good Ones. Use them now, before everyone else does and while they are wildly out of fashion.

To Daffodils	**Herrick**
Sir Patrick Spens	**Anon**
Against Idleness and Mischief	**Isaac Watts**
(How doth the little busy bee . . .)	
Loss of the 'Royal George'	**Cowper**
The Tyger	**Blake**
To Daffodils	**Wordsworth**
Lochinvar	**Scott**
The Lay of the Last Minstrel	**Scott**
The Rime of the Ancient Mariner	**Coleridge**
Bethgelert	**Spencer**
Bishop Hatto and the Rats	**Southey**
The Destruction of Sennacherib	**Byron**
Ozymandias	**Shelley**
No! (November)	**Hood**
Casabianca	**Hemans**
(The boy stood on the burning deck . . .)	
The May Queen	**Tennyson**

The Revenge	**Tennyson**

(At Flores in the Azores where Sir Richard
Grenville lay ...)

Break, break, break	**Tennyson**
The Old Navy	**Marryat**

(The Captain stood on the carronade ...)

Christmas Day in the Workhouse*	**Sims**
The Shooting of Dan McGrew	**Service**
Vitae Lampada	**Newbolt**
The Listeners	**De La Mare**
Sea Fever	**Masefield**

* Possibly the best poem ever written.

The English Cowpat School of Verse

There runs through English poetry a constant stream of verbal diarrhoea praising all things rural: cornfields, skylarks, meadows, rivers, brooks, cows, duckponds, molecatchers, horseflies, sexual deviants, nosey-parkers, gin-traps, etc. etc. Significantly, such poems have only come into existence in the last couple of hundred years, i.e. since most of us stopped living in the country. Nowadays, some misguided local authority has only to chop down a diseased tree for someone to write a poem and send it to the papers, and almost every furred or feathered creature or parasite (with the possible exception of skunk and tapeworm) has been the subject of a rapturous ode.

Poets of this school with the best yield are listed below:

Clare, John 1793-1864
Clare was a herd-boy, militiaman, vagrant, unsuccessful farmer and successful lunatic. He wrote wonderful poetry full of the buzzing of insects, the heat of noon, rush poles, hazel-nuts, ivied oaks and so on. Many hold that he wrote his greatest poems after he'd been certified. There's a Great Truth there, somewhere.

45

Blunden, Edmund 1896-1974

It has been said that 'Blunden's greatest service to poetry has been the researches into and discovery and publication of the hitherto unpublished poems of John Clare'. Blunden's own early poems were lavish in their praise of the pastoral, whether 'blotched with mildew', 'black scowling pond', 'cornered weasel', 'sunlit vale' or 'many centuried tree'.

Davies, William Henry 1871-1940

Author of *Autobiography of a Super Tramp*, though he lost a foot while jumping from one freight train to another, Davies wrote short poems, full of comedy (he said):

> Where bumble-bees, for hours and hours,
> Sit on their soft, fat, velvet bums,
> To wriggle out of hollow flowers . . .

De la Mare, Walter 1873-1956

It's probably best not to say anything yet about Walter de la Mare. Serves him right for writing about fairies and fancies and things called Tom Noddy. Almost entirely a 'punishment poet'.

Housman, Alfred Edward (points for knowing these names as he's always called 'A.E.') 1859-1936

It's still all right to talk about Housman because, although he wrote about cherry blossom, hawthorn, millstreams, nightingales, etc., he also wrote about people being hanged, battles, hard labour and all that.

Georgian Poets

A complete bluff of a name, **Georgian Poetry** is nothing to do with any George at all, but is the name given to a body of English verse composed from about 1910 to 1930, much of it of a pastoral, rural or rustic nature (see also – The English Cowpat School of Verse).

The poetry itself rapidly became very unfashionable,

although a grand bunch of people wrote it: **A.E. Hous-man**, **W.H. Davies**, **Walter de la Mare**, **Masefield**, **Victoria Sackville-West**, **Graves**, **Blunden**, and others. It was really the last flowering of English verse before it all went modern or whimsical, taking itself either too seriously or not seriously enough, like a mixture of Stockhausen and Spike Jones.

The surprising thing about the Georgian group is that it really was a group, with a real leader, Edward Marsh, one time Churchill's secretary at the Admiralty. The group achieved great popularity for a limited period, but was dealt a swift death blow by Eliot's *The Waste Land*.

T.S. Auden

Try to get as little involved as possible with the two literary 'giants' of the 20th century, **Auden** and **Eliot**. It's always exhausting to take on people who have 'given voice to the disillusionment of their generation', and the race to be best Auden/Eliot swot began ages ago so you're already miles behind. But if you want to compete, here's something to get you out of the starting blocks.

T.S. Eliot 1888-1963
Open by saying that Eliot suffered all his life from deracination (being torn up by the roots) and aboulia. Follow this by remarking on his study of Sanskrit and Pali. The only one of Eliot's poets that isn't a dreadful sweat to read is *The Love Song of Alfred J. Prufrock* (his earliest mature poem), and you can wax lyrical about "the mysterious interstices of this poem, its mixture of colloquialism and elegance, and its memorable ironies", ending by stating that "the portrait of enervation was executed with contradictory energy".

Eliot's most famous poem, *The Waste Land*, was written in Margate and Lausanne and published in 1922. It was thought outrageous at the time, but Eliot himself referred to it as 'just a piece of rhythmical grumbling'. It has been hailed as bringing together various kinds of despair – for lost youth, lost love, lost friendship, lost value, lost fountain pen, etc.

Eliot's other major work is the *Four Quartets*, and you get hundreds of points if you know their names: *Burnt Norton* (1935), *East Coker* (1940, *The Dry Salvages* (1941), and *Little Gidding* (1942).

W.H. Auden 1907-1973
Auden cherished the belief that he was of Icelandic origin, which makes you feel that he had a greater claim to deracination than Eliot. When he went to Christ Church, oxford, he confided in his tutor, Neville Coghill, that his ambition was to be a great poet – you could say that sort of thing in the mid 1920s and get away with it.

He was influenced by Eliot, and decided poems should be 'verbal artefacts'. He was also influenced by Homer Lane, and took as his theme for poetry 'the healing power of uninhibited love'. Like Eliot he became a teacher (the boys knew him as Uncle Wiz), and then spent the rest of his life making Very Important Decisions. He decided it was wrong to defend freedom against Fascism (though he did go to Spain as an ambulance driver for the Republicans). He decided to stay in the US with his great friend **Christopher Isherwood**, though unkind people said it was easier to fight Fascism (or not) from a distance. In fact, Auden left England for love, having met a young New York poet called **Chester Kallman**. They wrote the libretto for Stravinsky's *The Rake's Progress* together, but it was an unhappy relationship.

Say, loudly and confidently, that Auden wrote no decent poetry after leaving England, save *The Shield of Achilles* and *In Praise of Limestone* – he had a thing about rocks.

Auden was obsessively punctual, excessively funny in his youth, and liked to mock his religious faith – he often referred to the Almighty as 'Miss God'. In later life he had the horrors that he would fall down dead in his New York apartment and his body wouldn't be discovered for over a week. This was probably a ploy to have an interesting death and thus become a truly great poet. In fact, he died in Vienna on the 29th September 1973 after a very successful reading of his poems. It seems a little excessive as an encore.

Perhaps the bluffer's best approach when the conversation turns to Eliot and Auden is to say "What about Empson?" (**William Empson** 1906-1984 a contemporary of Eliot and Auden, who wrote two volumes of verse, *Poems* and *The Gathering Storm* (a title pinched by Churchill), which are really difficult, full of analytical argument and imagery drawn from Quantum Physics and Einstein's Theory of Relativity).

The BBC School

At one time **Louis MacNeice** and **George MacBeth**, did much to popularize poetry through broadcasting, but now the BBC takes a stronger line. It believes poetry is a minority sport. Every so often some contemporary poet with a slight speech impediment is taken down into a basement studio at Broadcasting House and allowed to stumble his or her way through ten minutes of metaphor encrusted tat, or an Oxbridge Don gives a talk entitled 'Hitherto Neglected Correspondence Between Gerard Manley Hopkins and the Metropolitan Water Board'. These ramblings may be broadcast eighteen months later on Radio 3, in between Acts 13 and 14 of a Hans Werner Henze opera. They then provoke a storm of quietude and a column and a half in *The Listener*.

'Twas not ever thus. Give a wry smile and mention **Alan Brownjohn**, **Peter Porter**, **Anthony Thwaite** and **Dylan Thomas**, fine poets all, who saw the radio as a means of disseminating verse and were allowed to use it.

The Ejaculatory School

This has been in existence for hundreds of years and will outlast Experimentalism, Birdyak and anything else the avant garde cares to invent.

Open any book of poetry and you will find small words of exhortation, amazement, shock or delight at the beginning of one line or another:

> Oh, how hideous it is   (**Ezra Pound**)

> O fie upon the virgin birds   (**Thomas Randolph**)

> Ah God! that it were possible   (**Tennyson**)

> Say! You've struck a heap of trouble
>   (**Robert Service**)

> Gush! – flush the man, the being with it, sour or
>   sweet   (**Gerard Manley Hopkins**)

> Ah what avails the sceptred race!
> Ah what the form divine   (**Walter Savage Landor**)

> O sylvan Wye! thou wanderer through the woods
>   (**Wordsworth**)

> Alas! regardless of their doom
> The little victims play   (**Gray**)

Some poets manage three ejaculations in one line:

> O Peace, O Dove, O shape of the Holy Ghost
>   (**Richard Watson Dixon**)

but there are others who base their whole output on these (usually) monosyllabic openings:

> But hark! the cry is Astur:
> And lo! the ranks divide;   (**Macaulay**)

Dr Johnson began his *Epitaph on Claudy Phillips, a Musician* as though about to admonish the poor deceased:

> Phillips!

John Betjeman

Betjeman used an enormous number of 'oh's, often at the beginnings of poems, but also broadened the Ejaculatory Vocabulary by including 'Huzza!', 'Look up!', 'Come on, come on', 'Hark!', 'Take me, Lieutenant!', 'Row like smoke!', 'Behold!', 'Swing up!', 'Swing down!', and some complete lines that only he could have written:

> Come, friendly bombs and fall on Slough

> Oh! full Surrey twilight! importunate band!
> Oh! strongly adorable tennis-girl's hand!

> Stop the trolley-bus, stop!

> Early Electric! With what radiant hope
> Men formed this many branched electrolier

> Return, return to Ealing,
> Worn poet of the farm!

> Oh where's mid-on? And what is silly point?
> Do six balls make an over? Help me, God!

Thomas Babington Macaulay

Macaulay relied heavily on O! and Ho!, but was also a keen Hark!-ist, and often took the precaution of starting a poem with 'Attend!', presumably conscious that his audience might well be about to go to sleep.

> Ho! strike the flagstaff deep, Sir Knight: ho!
>   scatter flowers fair maids:
> Ho! gunners fire a loud salute: ho! gallants,
>   draw your blades.

> Hark! hark! – What means the trampling
>   of horsemen on our rear?

> Lo! I will stand at thy right hand . . .

Point out that Macaulay's ejaculations are not in the same league as Betjeman's, being used merely to retain the metre of the line. For lo! it's trivial information of this kind that keeps the real expert at bay.

Edward Fitzgerald

Fitzgerald's most famous poem, the translation of *The Rubaiyat of Omar Khayyam of Naishapur*, begins with even less optimism as to its reception than Macaulay had:
    'Awake!',
as though the audience, or possibly the reader, is already asleep. (If you think it's impossible to read poetry and be asleep at the same time, you've either never taught English Literature, or you've been very lucky, or you've never read anything from the 18th century.)

Fitzgerald, like Macaulay, was an O! and Oh! man, but, being more sensuous, he was also fond of Ah!, as though smacking his lips, or her bottom. As befits the author of *The Rubaiyat*, Fitzgerald had a full range of ejaculations:

Ah, my Beloved, fill the cup* . . .

Lo! some we loved . . .

Ah, make the most of what we yet may spend . . .

Fools! your Reward is neither Here nor There!

Oh, come with old Khayyam . . .

Ah, fill the cup* . . .

Oh, Thou, who didst with Pitfall and with Gin** . . .

Alas, that Spring should vanish with the Rose!

Ah, Moon of my Delight . . .

*   Fitzgerald was also very fond of emptying the cup.
** Presumably this was what he liked to fill it with.

There are still people writing this sort of stuff today. You have been warned.

POEMS FOR ALL

It is impossible to avoid poetry; it is almost as ubiquitous as dog mess, and just as nasty to step in. Even if you stay resolutely at home, shut in a darkened room, it will come thudding through your letter box in the form of cards.

These verses represent Poetry for the Masses, the essence of which is the belief that trite sentiments are best immortalized in verse. Nobody would dream of translating the message of a greetings card into prose, but there are two mitigating circumstances:

1. Trying to find a new way of saying 'Happy Birthday' in verse is a bit like trying to find a new way of serving bangers and mash.
2. Writers of greetings card verses are working in the great tradition of the Poets Laureate – compiling verses for special occasions.

Poet Laureate is a title given to some ambitious rhymster who writes accessible verse that even members of the Royal Family and the Government can understand. For his great sin, he (it is always a 'he') is given a stipend of three groats a year and is charged with the duty of writing patriotic verse whenever the country does anything remotely embarrassing (diplomatic coup, Royal birth, going to war, clinching a trade contract with Taiwan, winning a bronze medal at the Olympics).

Of recent years the Poet Laureate has kept a lower and lower profile, and the present incumbent, **Ted Hughes**, seems to have decided, very sensibly, that his best bet in this capacity is to disappear from sight and print altogether.

Few Laureates ever wrote anything worthwhile, viz:

Along the electric lines the message came
'He is no better: he is much the same' . . .

from a poem about Edward VII's illness written by **Alfred Austin** (appointed 1892).

A notable exception is **Alfred, Lord Tennyson** (appointed 1850), the longest holder of the post, who could even turn national disasters into such glories as:

Half a league, half a league, / Half a league onward.
All in the valley of Death / Rode the six hundred.

Bluffers should bone up on a few unknown ones, such as **Nahum Tate** (appointed 1692, died 1715) whose most famous poem was in praise of Tea, **Colley Cibber** (1730, died 1757), an actor who also wrote plays of which Congreve said, 'they have in them things that were like wit, but in reality were not wit'; and **Thomas Wharton** (appointed 1785, died 1790) who revived the sonnet, and edited a book of verse called *The Oxford Sausage*.

William McGonigall, Poet and Tragedian

McGonigall is the world's finest bluffing poet ever, grossly and wickedly ignored until the 1950s. All his life he was the victim of hoaxes, practical jokes and leg-pulls, but his sublime muse rises above all this. Particular gems to look out for include the memorable trio of poems:

The Railway Bridge of the Silvery Tay
    Beautiful Railway Bridge of the Silvery Tay
    That has caused the Emperor of Brazil to leave
    His home far away, incognito in his dress,
    And view thee ere he passed along en route to
    Inverness . . .

The Tay Bridge Disaster
    Beautiful Railway Bridge of the Silv'ry Tay!
    Alas! I am very sorry to say
    That ninety lives have been taken away
    On the last Sabbath day of 1879
    Which will be remembered for a very long time . . .

and *An Address to the New Tay Bridge*
    Beautiful new railway bridge of the Silvery Tay . . .

AMERICAN POETRY

It's a good idea to make American poetry your bluffing speciality as there has been only two hundred years of it, if you discount the indigenous poetry of the Crow, Blackfeet, Apache, Sioux, etc.

The earliest recognisable poet from America was probably **Anne Bradstreet** (1612-1672), but the founding figures of American poetry are generally reckoned to be **Ralph Waldo Emerson** and **Edgar Allen Poe** (most American poets have three names). In 1837, Emerson marched into Harvard University and delivered an address called 'The American Scholar', the message of which was that nature and instinct are better guides for human behaviour than books and learning. It didn't go down well at the time, but Oliver Wendell Holmes later called it 'Our Intellectual Declaration of Independence'.

James Russell Lovell summed up **Poe** in the following couplet:

Here comes Poe with his Raven, like Barnaby Rudge,
Three fifths of him genius, two fifths sheer fudge.

Poe kept well away from long poems and from those that preached moral improvement. He also loathed **Henry Wadsworth Longfellow**'s rhythmic story telling (though *Hiawatha* is almost certainly the best known American poem in England).

Poe's poetical philosophy was simple:

Q. What is the most melancholy of topics?
A. Death.
Q. What is the most beautiful of topics?
A. A beautiful woman.
Q. What, therefore, is the best thing to write a poem about?
A. The Death of a Beautiful Woman.

Poe wrote lots.

Walt Whitman's most celebrated work is *Leaves of Grass*, which ran to some hundred and fifty poems written over a period of thirty years. His poetry is proud, audacious and pioneering, and a lot of it is sexually outspoken, which made Whitman very popular with other 19th century poets (Rossetti, Swinburne) and very unpopular with everyone else.

Unlike most poets, who are desperate to see their work in print, only two of **Emily Dickinson**'s poems were published during her life, and these without her consent. She died leaving over seventeen hundred poems and is reckoned a genius by many. Recognition came late, about seventy years after her death. You can be enthusiastic about her poetry, calling it lyrical, paradoxical, gnomic – but check that you know what 'gnomic' means (see Glossary).

Robert Frost began writing poetry when he was in his late thirties (around 1912), and his early works have an archaic touch ('She talks and I am fain to list'). Later his poetry became more powerful and awarded him four Pulitzer Prizes and forty four honorary degrees. Call him 'aphoristic' (see Glossary).

William Carlos Williams

The happy thing about Wiliiams is that he was a Cubist, Surrealist, Symbolist, Objectivist, Imagist, Lyricist poet, so you can say anything you like about him.

Ezra Pound

Pound was dismissed from his first job (Teacher of Roimace Philology at Wabash College) on suspicion of moral turpitude and 'Bohemian behaviour' – you can make what you like of that – and his life was one long slide into the unacceptable. He left the US and went to Italy, where he preached anti-Semitism and became a big hit on Radio Mussolini. After the Second World War he was tried for treason, but found unfit to plead, and was confined in a mental institution. Released in 1958, lived to the ripe old age of 87 and wrote hundreds of 'Cantos'. If you favour Pound, try to 'let the images fall into your memory without questioning the reasonableness of each at the moment; so that, at the end, a total effect is produced' (T.S. Eliot). If not, take a firm stand and declare that better poets have been locked away in mental institutions with less cause.

Allen Ginsberg once described his poetry as 'Angelical Ravings'. One time hero of the Beat Generation, there's hardly a line that doesn't mention 'madness', 'fix', 'narcotic haze', 'undressing', 'drunk', etc. If you rave about Ginsberg, you're likely to be met with blank stares by anyone under forty. If anyone over forty raves to you about Ginsberg, they've probably got a blank stare, but for a totally different reason.

Sylvia Plath wrote most of her poetry at four o'clock in the morning, which may account for the depression that most of it engenders. It is heavy stuff. Don't read it at four o'clock in the morning.

Dorothy Parker approached death with delightful wit, as in *Résumé*:

> Razors pain you;
> Rivers are damp;
> Acids stain you;
> And drugs cause cramp.
> Guns aren't lawful;
> Nooses give;
> Gas smells awful;
> You might as well live.

And live she did. It took Dorothy 74 years to drink herself to death, which is slow going for a poet.

There's one way to approach American poetry without having to read any of it (always the preferred way of approaching poetry), and still appearing an expert on the subject. Some of the slickest, liveliest and most moving verse from the States is to be found in the lyrics of songs. The names to remember above all are **Lorenz Hart** (of Rodgers and Hart), **E.Y. Harburg**, and **Ira Gershwin**. Books of their work have been published, showing, in the case of Hart especially, a massive, sophisticated and witty output. The great advantage is that here is an immense volume of poetry that you already know. The great difficulty is managing to recite these poems without bursting into song. Claim that the appeal is in the "wonderfully rhythmic quality of the verse" and in "the innovatory use of rhyme", e.g. **Cole Porter**'s:

> . . . flying so high/with some guy/in the sky/is my i/-dea of nothing to do . . .
>
> *I Get a Kick Out of You*

> . . . when you love your lover let/blue skies be your coverlet . . .
>
> *Mountain Greenery*

or the verse of Ira Gershwin's *Our Love is Here to Stay* written to the last song George Gershwin ever wrote, and in which Ira is mourning the death of a much loved brother. Avoid **Oscar Hammerstein II**.

The other American poets to try without hurting your brain are **e.e.cummings** (the man with the broken caps key) and **Ogden Nash** – author of that delightful ditty:
Shake, oh shake the ketchup bottle
None will come, and then a lottle.

THE CURRENT STATE

Bluffers should remember that the slim volume all the critics are raving about today may be on the 'remaindered' pile tomorrow. Never commit yourself to reading every issue of every poetry magazine (there are lots) or checking the poetry shelves of your local bookstore to make sure you haven't missed a new edition of Contemporary Afghan Poetry or The Use of Standard English, Creole and the Nation Language by Jean Binta Breeze and Fred d'Aguiar.

Let others sift through the bulging granaries of verse, sorting the less bad from the terrible. We know *now* that Brian Patten, Adrian Henri and Roger McGough have staying power – but not when it counted, twenty five years ago. We shall be well into the next century before we know who were the good poets of the 1980s and 1990s.

Currently, a great deal of attention is being paid to 'rap'. Raps are lengthy monologues, often performed with rhythm accompaniment, and dealing largely with rejection. Rap poets have broken new ground by rejecting the world before it rejects them. There is also a great surge of interest in Australian Aborigine and Arab poetry. If you want to show off, mutter something about the four major schools of Arab poetry – the Taf'ila Movement (Iraqi School) 1947-1957; the Majallat Shi'ir Movement (Syrian School) 1957-1967; the Huzairan Experience 1967-1982; and the Beirut Experience, 1982 onwards.

Faced with an expert who is parading superior knowledge of contemporary poets, the best thing for the bluffer is to be unstintingly admiring: "You're reading all these new apprentices? How brave! I'm afraid it will take me the rest of my life to do justice to the late medieval mnemonics." It's a pretty safe bet that the enthusiast won't know that by 'late medieval mnemonics' you mean *Green Grow the Rushes, O*.

GLOSSARY

Anapest: A dactyl flying backwards, e.g. de-de dum.

Aphorism: Any short, pithy statement into which much thought or observation is compressed. Therefore very rare.

Ballad: Simple poem of spirit in mercifully short verses and often easy to follow. Dates from the 15th century.

Blank Verse: Poetry written by poets too lazy to be bothered with rhymes, but who were good at counting up to ten. Invented by the Earl of Surrey (see – Poets and Death).

Couplet: Two lines of poetry, as in
> Auntie, did you hurt yourself, falling from that tree?
> Would you do it once again, please 'cos my friend
> here didn't see?
> > (*Ruthless Rhymes* – Harry Graham)

Dactyl: A metrical foot consisting of one long and two short syllables, e.g. dum de-de. Comes from the Greek for 'joints of the finger'.

Elegaic Distich: A couplet consisting of a hexameter and a pentameter:
> dum de de, dum de de, dum de de, dum de de, dum de de, dum dum,
> dum dum, dum dum, dum dum, dum dum, dum dum.

(It reads better if you use actual words.)

Elegy: Not the sort of poem to cause a rash, but a song of lamentation, often a funeral ode. You don't get many of them these days.

Elizabethan Sonnet: A rhyming scheme favoured by Shakespeare – abab/cdcd/efef/gg.

Gasometer: Measurement of sincerity in poetry.

Gnomic: Full of maxims (the slogans, not the machine guns). Sententious. Aphoristic.

Haiku: Japanese verse consisting of three lines of five, seven and five syllables respectively. The most famous classical haiku writer, was Basho.

Hexameter: A line of six metrical feet, usually five dactyls and a spondee, although you can have five spondees and one dactyl if you like – but never use a spondee on the fifth foot.

Iambic: Lines based on iambuses, that is feet consisting of a short followed by a long syllable – de **dum**.

Iconoclastic: What every poet would like to be – thumbing his or her nose at venerated images.

Jongleur: Reciter of licentious and merry metrical tales. As a profession it has always lacked career prospects.

Lay: A song sung by a minstrel.

Little Tich: Music Hall artist who wore two long feet or spondees.

Lyric: Short poem divided into stanzas or strophes, directly expressing the poet's own thoughts and sentiments. The suggestion is that all other poetry doesn't, and is therefore cribbed.

Metre: Any form of poetic rhythm: also, a unit of measurement that the British are still yards behind.

Minstrel: Individual who used to wander about in medieval times singing his own and other people's verse. Now happily defunct.

Neo: A term often misused – strictly, it means 'new', but it's often used to mean 'a bit like . . .'

Ode: Not as familiar in style as a song – more a rhymed lyric in the form of an address. All odes start 'O!', except those by Keats and Cyril Fletcher.

Panegyric: Boot-licking.

Pentameter: Five foot line of verse. English heroic pentameters had ten syllables – dum dum dum dum dum dum dum dum dum dum – and so were jolly dull dull dull dull . . .

Petrachan Sonnet: A rhyming scheme invented by Petrarch who was a great fan of Swedish minstrels, hence: abba/abba, followed by two or three other rhymes in the remaining six lines of the Sonnet.

Rhapsodes: Ancient performers of poetry who very sensibly carried big sticks. Nowadays it's people who have to listen to poetry who should be armed.

Slim volume: Twee name given to a book of poetry. Books of contemporary poetry are kept slim because nobody really wants to read much contemporary poetry.

Sonnet: A poem of fourteen lines.

Spondee: Metrical foot of two long syllables, e.g. dum dum.

Stanza: A verse.

Strophe: A complicated Greek metrical construction that usually went wildly wrong, hence 'catastrophe'.

Trochee: The opposite of an iambus, e.g. dum de.

Troubadour: Essentially a lyric poet from southern France, eastern Spain or northern Italy who sang songs of chivalry and gallantry in the Provencal language. Most troubadours were taken to the pass of Roncesvalles to be wiped out.

THE AUTHOR

Nick Yapp first became aware of poetry when he had to learn some as a punishment at school. Much moved by the experience, and swamped with thoughts of Love, Suffering, Death and Toffees, he subsequently wrote a great deal of verse, but has stopped all that since he became a grown-up and retired from teaching to become a full-time writer.

His favourite poets are Keats, Betjeman, Harry Graham and (most of all) William McGonigall. He has found it wise to keep quiet about all this, for poetry lovers are not much respected in Catford, where he lives with his wife, son, VISA card, low level alcohol, vinyl flooring and poetry books that he bought thirty years ago in case he was given more punishment.

THE BLUFFER'S GUIDES®

Available at £1.99 and (new titles* £2.50) each:

Accountancy	Maths
Advertising	Modern Art
Antiques	Motoring
Archaeology	Music
Astrology & Fortune Telling	The Occult
Ballet	Opera
Bird Watching	Paris
Bluffing	Philosophy
British Class	Photography
Chess	Poetry
Champagne*	P.R.
The Classics	Public Speaking
Computers	Publishing
Consultancy	Racing
Cricket	Rugby
Doctoring	Secretaries
The European Community	Seduction
Finance	Sex
The Flight Deck	Skiing*
Golf	Small Business*
The Green Bluffer's Guide	Teaching
Japan	Theatre
Jazz	University
Journalism	Weather Forecasting
Literature	Whisky
Management	Wine
Marketing	World Affairs

These books are available at your local bookshop or newsagent, or can be ordered direct. Prices and availability are subject to change without notice. Just tick the titles you require and send a cheque or postal order for the value of the book, and add for postage & packing:

UK including BFPO — £1.00 per order
OVERSEAS including EIRE – £2.00 per order

Ravette Books, P O Box 11, Falmouth, Cornwall TR10 9EN.